LORD, TEACH US TO PRAY

Tom Harmon

Ajoyin Publishing, Inc
P.O. Box 342 Three Rivers, MI 49093
888.273.4JOY
www.ajoyin.com

Lord, Teach Us To Pray

ISBN: 978-1-60920-016-9
Printed in the United States of America
©2011 by Tom Harmon
All rights reserved

Library of Congress Cataloging-in-Publication Data

Edited by Bob English
Front Cover photo by Steve McCormick

Ajoyin Publishing, Inc.
P.O. 342
Three Rivers, MI 49093
www.ajoyin.com

First published 11/10/2009
978-1-4490-3965-3 (e)
978-1-4490-3964-6 (sc)

Please direct your inquiries to admin@ajoyin.com

Contents

Foreword: vii

Preface: ix

Introduction to Prayer xi

Chapter One: Watch and Pray.................................... 1

Chapter Two: Two Secrets to One Hour..................... 11

Chapter Three: The Blessing of Private Prayer 31

Chapter Four: Power in Prayer 45

Chapter Five: Preventative Prayer 59

Chapter Six: Prayers that Sanctify............................ 69

Chapter Seven: Finishing Well................................. 79

Foreword:

I want to leave a legacy of faith to my wife, children, grandchildren, and the people God brings within my sphere of influence. I hope that writing a series of books on consecrated living will aid me in this endeavor as well as strengthen my own faith.

Preface:

A consecrated life is one that is devoted to the worship and service of God. It is my personal belief that as a person grows in the grace and the knowledge of the Lord Jesus Christ, he develops an inner desire for consecrated living. Consecrated people still experience failure, but they have matured sufficiently to know how to trust God and benefit through their failures and continue on in their journey of faith. In Philippians 3:12, the Apostle Paul made it clear that he had not arrived at perfection: "Not as though I had already attained, either were already perfect; *but I follow after*, if that I may apprehend that for which also I am apprehended of Christ Jesus." As I attempt to write about the consecrated life, I will be writing from the perspective of one that is following after Christ Jesus, and not as one who has arrived.

Introduction to Prayer

Shortly after committing my life to Christ I heard a powerful sermon on prayer. I was both convicted and inspired to learn to pray. It took me ten years to learn *to pray,* and it will take me the rest of my life to learn *how to pray.* I have been praying now for the past twenty years. I have found it to be the greatest expression of my faith, and I believe that it is true for all Christians. Prayer has changed my life more than any of the spiritual graces, for nothing should be done without prayer. It's the one thing you can't overdose on. It involves labor and yet it becomes a supreme delight. You can pray at all times, and in all places. Few in heaven will be heard to say, "I wish I would have watched more television", but many may be heard to say, "I wish I would have prayed more". Lord, teach us to pray.

Chapter One:

Watch and Pray

Prayer is one of the great mysteries of God. What a joy just to ponder the privilege of what it means to have access into the very presence of God. "By whom also we have access by faith into this grace in which we stand, and rejoice in the hope of the glory of God" (Rom. 5:2). Because of our high priest, the Lord Jesus, we can come boldly to the very throne of God's grace. "Let us therefore come boldly unto the throne of grace, that we may obtain mercy, and find grace to help in time of need" (Heb. 4:16). If we are ever going to know God, we will need his help. Prayer is one of the great helps in our pursuit to knowing him.

Jesus, our example, was often in prayer. He prayed publicly but most importantly he prayed privately. Luke 11:1 records that after he had finished praying his disciples came to him and asked him to teach them to pray. Had they never prayed? Were they unfamiliar with the prayers in the Psalms? As children in synagogue school, had they slept through the rabbinical prayers? No, I think their request came from hearts convicted of their own prayerlessness. They didn't a.. Jesus to teach them "*how to pray*"; they just wanted him to teach them "to pray". Learning *how to pray* always follows learning *to pray.*

Prayer should be the initial response to everything we do. When we live in an attitude of prayer, speaking with God is automatic. In everything we do, we learn not to panic, but to pray. "Be anxious for nothing; but in everything by prayer and supplication with thanksgiving let your requests be made known unto God" (Phil. 4:6). We are learning *to pray* when we realize that prayer is acknowledging our absolute dependence on God. Praise God, I have learned *to pray.* Now, I can spend the rest of my life learning *how to pray.* My desire is that this book will be of some help in your personal journey of faith and prayer.

Prayer is something that can be, and should be, a primary part of everything we do. All too often we think of prayer simply as asking God to do the supernatural on our behalf. Do you remember the case of Hezekiah and his sickness? Isaiah 38 records that the prophet Isaiah had just told the King to get his house in order, because he is going to die. Hezekiah prays and God grants him an extension of fifteen years. Another example is recorded in Acts 12. The apostle Peter is in prison and most likely awaiting execution the following day. The church gathers and prays without ceasing. God sends an angel to the jail and Peter is miraculously freed. These are great and powerful answers to prayer which encourage us to pray. Yet, I think God in his sovereign omniscience, has chosen an even greater and more powerful work of prayer for us today. I believe our work of everyday prayer is involved in the eternal work of saving and sanctifying souls. Therefore, in introduction, I would like to consider some thoughts from Matthew 26:41 "Watch and pray, that ye enter not into temptation: the spirit indeed is willing, but the flesh is weak."

This verse shares several important steps on the journey of learning *to pray*. The first step is acknowledging that the spirit indeed is willing but the flesh is weak. It was true when Jesus spoke to his disciples in the garden of Gethsemane, and it is true for the disciples of Christ today. When a person has the Spirit of the living God dwelling within him, he has a desire to pray. When the Spirit of God comes to dwell in a person, he brings with him a desire for the things of God. Prayer strengthens the divine nature and aids the believer in the maturing process. Through prayer we take part in the power of God. "According as his divine power hath given unto us all things that pertain unto life and godliness, through the knowledge of him that has called us to glory and virtue: By which are given unto us exceedingly great and precious promises: that by these ye might be partakers of the divine nature, having escaped the corruption that is in the world through lust" (2 Pet. 1:3-4). The Spirit who indwells us surely brings with him a desire to pray, but we face the same old problem Peter, James, and John faced, the flesh is weak. Not only is it weak, it is incapable of true spiritual prayer. Even sincere Christians who desire to be spiritual can easily be distracted, daydream, or fall asleep. In chapter two I will share some things that have helped me stay awake and stay focused.

WATCH <u>AND</u> PRAY, NOT WATCH <u>OR</u> PRAY

Jesus shared words of wisdom with his disciples. Since the spirit was willing but the flesh was weak, they were to "watch and pray." He didn't tell them to just watch, or just pray, he said, "watch and pray." The word watch means to be vigilant, or awake. This word can safely be used metaphorically and applied to many areas of Christian responsibility. For instance, a person should study for an exam and pray that God would help them remember the material. He shouldn't just study and not pray, neither should he just pray and not study. Unfortunately, I think some of the latter has taken place in my own life. We don't just invite people to church, we pray for God to work in their lives and remove all their excuses. When they accept our invitation and come, we pray that we will be sensitive, and know how to properly treat them. We pray they would have ears to hear what the Spirit would say to them. We don't just pray and we don't just invite. We do both. We consciously and vigilantly watch and pray. This approach brings reasonableness to the Christian journey. When understood, it broadens into almost every area of our lives.

We train up our children in the way they should go and earnestly pray that they would walk in the ways of the Lord. Many parents raise their children the best they can, yet they fail to labor in prayer for them. Some parents pray for them to turn out right but neglect proper guidance in the ways of the Lord. Watch and pray is not an 'either-or' command. Watch and pray involves both conscious vigilance and praying. In this context it involves prayer and nurturing instruction. With Nehemiah we also say, "Nevertheless we made our prayer unto God, and set a watch against them day and night, because of them" (Neh. 4:9). Please, make wise choices with regard to the safety of your children and beseech God for their protection as well.

We don't just pray for good health while sitting around eating garbage food; neither do we just eat healthy food with regular exercise and cast prayer aside. We may walk the narrow way but we will never walk it very long without prayer. Watch and pray. Both are essential to lasting success. Good health is not always a sign of spiritually. It may be God has a different design in his sovereign plan for our lives. Even so, we pray for good health as we are attentive to our lifestyle. "Beloved, I wish above all things that thou mayest prosper and be in health even as thy soul prospersth" (3 John 2).

You may have attended seminars on marriage and had good marriage counseling. You may possibly have read some tremendous books and implemented some sound Biblical principals from the things you have learned. These are all good, but without prayer we can never move into the caliber of marriage God intended. On the other hand if you think you can pray yourself into a godly marriage while being unforgiving, proud, and selfish you are equally in error. Watch and pray means that we do the right things as we acknowledge our absolute dependence on God in prayer. "In all thy ways acknowledge him, and he shall direct thy paths" (Prov. 3:6). I might add that many a marriage problem could have been resolved and divorce avoided if the couple would have began praying together as little as three times a week.

It's So Easy to Forget

I think good and godly people sometimes forget to pray. Even those saints who are given to prayer find it hard to remember. For whatever reason, possibly just the weakness of our flesh, we forget. I think part of the curse is that we forget what we should remember and remember what we should forget. Scripture records both godly men and women who just forgot. There is no Biblical record of either Adam or Eve praying before they ate from the tree of the knowledge of good and evil.

Joshua was a godly man. His prayer mentor was Moses. Moses was a man who knew how to seek the Lord's face in prayer. When Joshua was leading the nation of Israel into the promise land, he prayed. When they crossed the Jordon River, Jericho had already fallen, Ai had been prayed through, and the fear of God was on the land of Canaan. The Gibeonites were the next to be conquered. However, they planned to deceive Israel with the story that they were from a long distance away. They brought the evidence of moldy bread, old wine skins, and worn out clothes. Joshua and the leaders of Israel fell for their deception. They believed their story and swore an oath that the Gibeonites would not be harmed. God had said to destroy all the inhabitants of the land. "[But] the [leaders of Israel] took of their provisions, and asked NOT counsel at the mouth of the Lord. And Joshua made peace with them, and made a league with them, and let them live; and the princes of the congregation swore unto them" (Josh. 9:14-15). All throughout Israel's history the Gibeonites brought them nothing but trouble, because Joshua had forgotten to pray.

David was a man after God's own heart, yet there is no Biblical record of David praying before his first attempt at bringing the Ark into Jerusalem. A man by the name of Uzzah died when he tried to steady the Ark as it was improperly being transported on an ox cart. (2 Sam. 6)

David's close friend, the prophet Nathan, forgot to pray before giving David the green light on building the temple. "And Nathan said to the king, "Go, do all that is in thine heart; for the Lord is with thee" (2 Sam.7:3). Later that night the word of the Lord came to Nathan making it clear that David was not to build his house. I don't think Nathan omitted prayer intentionally, he just forgot.

Again, there is no Biblical record that David prayed when he heard the news that Nahash the king of the Ammonites had died. He just sent emissaries to his son Hanun to comfort him in his loss. Hanun sent David's emissaries back in shame. Did David pray then? There is no record of it. Nor is there record that he prayed before he told Joab to go destroy the Ammonites. In this situation David should have led the battle, but because he didn't pray and didn't go, he was set up perfectly for the weakness of the flesh. The scene with Bathsheba quickly followed. 2 Samuel 11 records the fallout of that event.

In 1 Peter 3 Sarah is referred to as a holy woman of old, with chaste conduct and a genuine reverence for God and her husband. Yet, there is no Biblical record that she prayed prior to offering Hagar to Abraham. The results of her prayerless scheme are still being felt in the world today. I wonder how much different history would look if certain people had remembered to pray.

There are numerous examples, but I want to close with one more from the life of a godly king, King Asa. "And

Asa did that which was good and right in the eyes of the Lord his God. For he took away the altars of the foreign gods, and the high places, and broke down the images, and cut down the idols, and he commanded Judah to seek the Lord God of their fathers, and to do the law and the commandment"(2 Chr. 14:2-4). When Asa faced Zerah the Ethiopian and his army of one million, "[He] cried unto the Lord his God, and said, Lord, it is nothing with thee to help, whether with many, or with them who have no power. Help us, O Lord our God, for we rest on thee, and in thy name we go against this multitude. O Lord, thou art our God, let not man prevail against thee" (2 Chr. 14:11). God heard his prayer and they destroyed the invading army. They never heard from them again. Later, when Asa was older, his foot became sore and it was getting worse. He called the physicians but he forgot to pray. It cost him his life. "And Asa in the thirty and ninth year of his reign was diseased in his feet until his disease was very great; yet in his disease he sought not to the Lord but the physicians" (2 Chr. 16:12). Watch and pray! Call the doctor and pray! Don't just pray and don't just call the doctor. Remember, it's so easy to forget.

CHAPTER TWO:

TWO SECRETS TO ONE HOUR

"And he cometh unto his disciples, and findeth them asleep, and saith unto Peter, What, could ye not watch with me one hour?" (Mt. 26:40). Most Christians will agree that it is easier to sing the old hymn "Sweet Hour of Prayer" than it is to pray for an hour. Is it possible for a Christian to pray for an hour? Is it possible for a Christian to pray for an hour a day? Would this be a reasonable goal or something meritorious, reserved only for the most spiritual of Christians? Since prayer is a learning process, I believe we can learn to pray for an hour and that it can become a sweet hour. In this chapter I would like to share two secrets I've found useful in praying for one hour.

MY FAVORITE DEFINITION OF PRAYER

Prayer is many things; it is contact with deity, it is entering into the presence of the almighty God, it is taking out of our hands that which we cannot do and placing it into his hands only that which he can do. My personal favorite definition of prayer is found in scripture. "But without faith it is impossible to please him; for he that cometh to God must believe that he is, and that he is the rewarder of them that diligently seek him" (Heb. 11:6). Prayer is coming to God and believing he is there. Prayer is one of the Christians greatest expressions of faith.

Secret #1 A Time and A Place

1 Thessalonians 5:17 tells us that we are to pray at all times. One will soon find, however, that it is hard to learn to pray at all times without having the discipline of praying at a specific time or times. David wrote, "Evening, and morning, and at noon, will I pray, and cry aloud: and he shall hear my voice" (Ps. 55:17). David knew if he was to have any success in his prayer life he needed to establish a time when he would retreat and be alone with God in prayer. His scheduled times of prayer laid the necessary foundation to a continuous attitude of dependence on God.

The place can be either public or private. Jesus referred to the temple, a place of public worship, as a house of prayer. Jesus also knew the value of private prayer. He taught the multitudes saying, "And when thou prayest, thou shalt not be as the hypocrites are: for they love to pray standing in the synagogues and at the corners of the streets, that they may be seen by men. Verily I say unto you, they have their reward. But thou, when thou prayest, enter into thy closet, and when thou hast shut thy door, pray to thy Father which is in secret; and thy Father which seeth in secret shall reward thee openly" (Mt. 6:5-6).

"To everything there is a season, and a time for every purpose under the heaven" (Eccl. 3:1). When I first pondered this verse in regards to prayer, I realized that if I did not have a specific time at which I prayed, a time in which I set all else aside, it would be as much as if I said to God, I don't have time to pray. I knew I needed a time and the Lord spoke to my heart from the Psalms. "My voice shalt thou hear in the morning, O Lord: in the morning will I direct my prayer unto thee, and will look up" (Ps. 5:3). Jesus himself prayed in the morning. "And in the morning, rising up a great while before day, he went out, and departed into a solitary place, and there prayed" (Mk.1:35). I chose 5:00am because it was the quietest and would have fewer distractions. I chose the basement because it was cooler and I wouldn't be as apt to fall asleep. Over the course of the next 10 years I would build a small prayer room in the corner of the basement. My children wrote out prayer verses and hung them on the walls. I memorized them as well as read a number of books on prayer. There were no windows in my prayer room and I chose to pray in the dark. One time I determined to pray for thirty minutes. I turned off the light and prayed for everything I could think of. Being quite confident I had succeeded I turned on the light and looked at my watch.

A little over five minutes had passed and needless to say I was quite discouraged. Though that decade seemed to me to produce little measurable progress toward prayer, it was not at all wasted. I learned much about waiting on the Lord and meditation. I learned how to be still and know that He is God and I am not. I gradually learned a secret that would change my prayer life forever. My wife and I came across it together as we began to share the prayers that we were praying for our children.

Secret # Two – Pray Categorically

One morning I asked my wife, Joyce, what she was praying for our children. She listed three or four things and said she was praying them everyday. I told her of two things I was praying. We combined our list and began to pray them daily. Before long we were adding other petitions until we had sixteen things we were praying daily. This gave me the structure that was so lacking in my prayers. I began to pray for others in the same organized categorical way. I had certain missionaries I prayed for everyday as well as, pastors and churches, friends and relatives, politicians and governmental agencies. I prayed for the lost and people I had been witnessing to. Within a year I had developed a strategy that was working. My wife and I would pray together every night and when I woke in the morning I would begin my private prayers.

The first moments of my prayer are given to praise, adoration, worship and thanksgiving. I then ask the Holy Spirit to help me in my prayers. "Likewise the Holy Spirit also helpeth our infirmities: for we know not what we should pray for as we ought: but the Spirit himself maketh intercession for us with groanings which cannot be uttered. And he that searcheth the hearts knoweth what is the mind of the Spirit, because he maketh intercession for the saints according to the will of God" (Rom. 8:26-27).

I Pray for My Own Soul First

I then move into praying for my own soul. This may and oftentimes does include confession and cleansing. I pray about the events of the day, whether it is a travel day, study day, preaching day, or a family day. I have no desire for a prayerless ministry regardless of what type of ministry it may be. I then take my stand against the world, the flesh and the devil. I put on all my armor and take up all my weapons. The following is a sample of this portion of my morning prayer, what I pray, and the scriptural reasons as to why.

Arena #1: The Flesh - Yielding Rights

"He that hath no rule over his own spirit is like a city that is broken down and without walls" (Prov. 25:28).

I choose today to die to self, to put off the old man and put on the new, to take up my cross and follow you (Lu 9:23, Col. 3:9-10). I choose to do this because I know that it is the refusal to die to self that makes me miserable.

I YIELD ...

1. The right to be appreciated, (Lu. 17:11-19)
2. The right to be right, (I Cor. 6:7-8, 1 Pet. 2:19-20)
3. The right to be heard, (1 Pet. 3:10-12, Jas. 3:1-10)
4. The right to nurse my hurts, (1 Pet. 5:7, Mt. 18:21-22, Ps. 130:3)
5. The right to privacy, (Lu. 9:12)
6. The right to leisure, (Mk. 6:30-33)
7. The right to defend myself, (Lu. 23:9)
8. The right to be needed, (2 Tim. 4:16-17, Ps. 8:3-4)
9. The right to good health, (2 Tim. 4:20, Job 2:10, 1 Pet. 4:12-13)
10. The right to financial security, (Acts 3:6, 1 Cor. 9:16-18)
11. The right to my schedule, (1 Th. 2:18, Gal. 4:4, Acts 1:7)
12. The right to friends, (Ps. 38:11, 41:9, Prov. 18:24)
13. The right to success in the ministry, (2 Cor. 4:7-11, John 1:10)
14. The right to be forgiven, (Mt. 6:12)
15. The right to be understood, (Mk. 8:14-21)
16. The right to be accepted, (John 1:11, 1 Pet. 4:19)

17. The right to pleasure, (Phil. 2:3)
18. The right to independence, (1 Cor. 6:19-20)
19. The right to be respected, (1 Cor. 4:13)
20. The right to my future plans, (2 Tim. 4:6, Jas. 4:13-15)
21. The right to things, (Lu. 12:20-21, Jas. 5:2-5)
22. The right to my expectations, (Ps. 62:5)
23. The right to control, (Eph. 5:18)
24. The right to my reputation, (Phil. 2:7)
25. The right to eat carelessly, (1 Cor. 9:23-27, Prov. 23:2)
26. The right to complain, (Phil. 2:14, Ex. 16:7-12)
27. The right to vengeance, (Rom. 12:19)
28. The right to comfort, (2 Cor. 4:16-18, 6:5)
29. The right to quit, (Prov. 24:16, 2 Tim. 4:7, Lu. 9:62)
30. The right to be angry, (Gen. 4:5-7, John 4:9, Prov. 16:32)
31. The right to relationships, (I Cor 9:5)
32. The right to understand, (Prov. 3:5-6, Isa. 55:8-9)

Arena #2: The World - In It but Not Of It

I choose today to be crucified to the world. God forbid that I should glory, save in the cross of our Lord Jesus Christ, by whom the world is crucified unto me and I unto the world (Gal. 6:14).

I don't want to love the world neither the things that are in the world, but set my affections on things above, where Christ sitteth on the right hand of God (1 John 2:15-17, Col. 3:2, Mt. 6:33).

I don't want to follow the philosophies of this world, but rather have the mind of Christ (Col. 2:8, Phil. 2:5-8).

I don't want to be conformed to this world, but I want to be conformed to the image of Christ (Rom. 12:2, 8:29, Gal. 4:19).

I don't want to walk according to the course of this world, but I want to walk in the Spirit (Eph. 2:2, Gal. 5:16).

For Jesus has said that in the world you will have tribulations, but be of good cheer, I have overcome the world, and what is the victory that overcomes the world, even our faith. For I want to walk by faith today and not by sight (John 16:33, 1 John 5:4, 2 Cor. 5:7).

ARENA #3: THE DEVIL - RESISTING THE ENEMY

I take my position along with other saints in resisting the devil (1 Pet. 5:8-9). Lord,

I pray that you would deny him any permission to assault me or my family today. I pray that every evil desire he has, you would turn back upon his own wicked head a thousand fold. If in your sovereign design you allow him to assault, I pray in advance that my faith would not fail (Lu. 22:31-32). I pray that you would not allow me to be deceived but discerning what the will of the Lord is, and to do it with all my heart (Rev. 20:10, Phil 2:13, Rom. 8:29). I pray that you would lead me not into temptation but deliver me from the evil one (Mt. 6:13).

I THANK YOU:

> * that Jesus came into the world to destroy the works of the devil, (1 John 3:8)

> * that because we are your children, we have overcome them, because greater is he that is in you than he that is in the world, (I John 2:14, 4:4)

> * that he that is begotten of God, God keeps and the wicked one touches him not, (1 John 5:18)

> * that you have written unto us, and we can be strong in your word and overcome the wicked one, (1 John 2:13)

> * that we are complete in him, who is the head of all principalities and powers, (Col. 2:10)

> * that your Son spoiled all principalities and powers, making a public spectacle of them stripping them of their rank and their power, all by himself at the cross, (Col. 2; 15)

* for delivering us from the power of darkness and translating us into the kingdom Of your dear Son, (Col. 1:13)

* that you, the God of peace shall bruise Satan under our feet shortly, (Rom 16:20)

* that the devil that deceived them will one day be cast into the lake of fire and brimstone where the beast and false prophet are and they shall be tormented day and night for ever and ever, (Rev. 20:10)

* that Satan never had a thing on Jesus, and that the prince of this world is already judged, (John 14:30, John 16:11)

These three arenas of conflict are listed for us in Ephesians 2:2-3 as well as in James 3:14-15. To be forewarned in scriptures is to be forearmed in Christian practice.

I Put on the Armor

I then pray on my armor and take up my weapons. This is my appropriation by faith of what I already have in Christ. (Eph. 6:10-18)

I want to be strong in the Lord and the power of his might so I put on by faith all the armor that you have provided me.

I PUT ON...

the girdle (belt) of truth. I want to speak truth today, (Eph. 4:25), because Jesus is truth, (John 14:6), his Spirit is truth, (John 14:17), his word is truth, (John 17:17), and the church is the pillar and ground of truth (1 Tim. 3:15). When I know the truth, the truth will always set me free (John 8:32).

I PUT ON...

the breastplate of righteousness, not having my own righteousness, which is after the law but the righteousness of God which is by faith of Christ Jesus (Phil. 3:9). Lord uphold me today by the right hand of your righteousness (Isa. 41:10, Ps. 48:10).

I PUT ON...

the sandals of peace and want to be a peacemaker today (Mt. 5:9). I pray the peace of God that passes all understanding will keep my heart and mind today (Phil. 4:7). Oh Lord I want you, the Prince of Peace, to rule and reign in every area of my life today (Isa. 9:6).

I TAKE UP...

the shield of faith, which is obedience to the word of God. For thou, oh Lord, art a shield for me, my glory and the lifter up of my head (Ps. 3:3). I pray that you would encompass me and my family today, as the mountains encompass Jerusalem, so encompass us as a shield (Ps. 125:2).

I PUT ON...

the helmet of salvation, refusing to receive thoughts that are contrary to your character. I bring every thought into captivity and obedience to the Lordship of Jesus Christ (2 Cor. 10:5). I want my mind to be stayed upon you (Isa. 26:3).

I Take up the Weapons

"For though we walk in the flesh, we do not war after the flesh. For the weapons of our warfare are not carnal, but mighty through God to the pulling down of strongholds" (2 Cor. 10:3-4).

I take up ...

> **THE SWORD** of the Spirit, which is the word of God, (Eph. 6:17) and grasp it   tightly with the powerful hand of
>
> **PRAYER** (Eph. 6:18). I do this in the
>
> **NAME ,** (Lu. 10:17, Phil. 2:10), and through the
>
> **BLOOD**, of the Lord Jesus Christ (Rev. 12:11). Always
>
> **PRAISING,** (1 Sam. 16:23),
>
> **PERSERVERING**, (Eph. 6:18), and seeking
>
> **GODLY COMRADES** (2 Tim. 4:19-21). Knowing that by the

WORD of our **TESTIMONY,** (Rev. 12:11), and the powerful commodities of

GRACE, (Jas. 4:6-7, 2 Cor. 9:8),

FASTING, (Mk. 9:29),

HUMILITY, (1 Pet. 5:5-6, Jas. 4:6-10),

WORSHIP, (Mt. 4:8-11, John 4:23-24),

A GOOD CONSCIENCE, (1 Tim. 1:5, 19),

MORAL PURITY, (1 Th. 4:3-7),

SERVING, (Lu. 22:27),

GRATEFULNESS, (1 Th. 5:18),

SELF DENIAL, (Lu. 9:23),

GOOD WORKS, (1 Pet. 3:10-12),

THE **JOY OF MY SALVATION,** (Ps. 51:12, 1 Pet. 1:8),

A WILLINGNESS TO FIGHT, (2 Cor. 8:12, 1 Tim. 6:12), and

THE PROCLAMATION OF THE GOSPEL, I seek to live for you today.

This section usually takes about somewhere between twenty or thirty minutes. I find a great blessing in praying these scriptures and many others that often come into this section of my prayers.

I Pray for My Family Next

I thank God for my precious wife, our children, grandchildren, and parents. I see my family not only as my ministry but also as my credentials for any additional ministry. Christ said he would build his church. He also loved the church and gave himself for it. In these two ways Christ is our example. We as men should love our wives as Christ loves his bride. Praying for my wife and family is, one of the greatest ways in following Christ example in building up my family.

"While I was with them in the world, I kept them in thy name: those that thou gavest me I have kept and none of them is lost, but the son of perdition; that the scriptures might be fulfilled" (John 17:12). "And for their sakes I sanctify myself, that they also might be sanctified through the truth" (John 17:19). These two verses come from what is known as the high priestly prayer of Jesus for his disciples. It seems like a good pattern in praying for my own family. I want my preaching ministry to be an overflow of what God is doing in my family. I don't want to stand in the pulpit and tell others about the power of Christ to change their lives and not be experiencing his changing power in my own life. I make it a point to pray for them by name everyday and any specific needs I become aware of. This area takes a good portion of my morning prayer.

As I mentioned at the beginning of this chapter, Joyce and I got started in categorical praying by praying for our children. I would like to include our original 16 things as well as a few additions we have made since becoming grandparents.

SIXTEEN THINGS WE PRAY
FOR OUR CHILDREN

1. Their Salvation, (Heb. 2:3, Phil. 2:12)

2. Their Mate, (Deut. 7:3-4, Phil. 2:1-4)

3. That they would fall in love with God's word, (Ps. 119:97, 165)

4. That God would keep them from the evil one, (John 17:15, Mt. 6:13)

5. That they would have a conscience void of offence before God and man, (Acts 24:16, 1 Tim. 1:5, 19)

6. That their character would be more valuable to them than their credentials, (2 Pet. 1:3-10)

7. That they would stand up for what is right even if it means standing alone, (Dan. 3:16-18, 2 Tim. 4:16-17)

8. That they would be kept from the love of money, (1 Tim. 6:6-12)

9. That they would be kept morally pure, (1 Th. 4:3-7, 1 Tim. 5:22)

10. That they would have the heart of a servant, (John 13:2-15, 2 Tim. 2:24-25)

11. That eternity would be in their hearts, (1 Tim. 6:12, Isa. 57:15)

12. That sin would always be distasteful to them and they would be broken easily over their sin, (Heb. 11:25, Ps. 51:17)

13. That they would always love each other, (1 John 3:11, 4:11, John 13:35)

14. That they would trust God with their parents and not allow rebellion to set in, (Prov. 3:5-6, Eph. 6:1-2, 1 Sam. 15:23)

15. Regardless the hardship, may they never become bitter against God, (Job 2:10, 1 Pet. 4:12)

16. That our boys would be glad to be boys and our girls be glad to be girls, (Ps. 139:13-18)

"And it was when the days of their feasting were finished, that Job sent and sanctified them, and rose up early in the morning and offered burnt offerings according to the number of them all: for Job said, it may be that my sons have sinned, and cursed God in their hearts, thus did Job continually" (Job1:5-6). It was Job's custom or habit to pray for his children daily. I think it is a good custom to follow.

Many of these things we now pray for our grandchildren as well as some new things.

1. That no evil would befall them or any plague comes near their dwelling, (Ps. 91: 10)

2. That all our children would be taught of the Lord and great would be the peace of our children, (Isa. 54:13-14)

3. That no weapon formed against them would ever prosper, (Isa. 54:17)

4. That they would have knowledge and good judgment, (Phil. 1:9)

5. That they would seek the Lord with all their hearts, (Ps. 34:10)

I Pray for Our Leaders

"I exhort therefore, that, first of all, supplications, prayers, intercessions, and giving of thanks, be made for all men; for kings, and for all that are in authority; that we may lead a quiet and peaceable life in all godliness and honesty. For this is good and acceptable in the sight of God our Savior; who will have all men to be saved, and to come unto the knowledge of the truth. For there is one God, and one mediator between God and men, the man Christ Jesus; who gave himself a ransom for all, to be testified in due time" (1 Tim. 2:1-6).

Based on this scripture I pray for our president and a number of other governmental officials everyday. I pray that all the Christians in government would stand for truth and righteousness. I pray that God in his mercy would send revival to America once again. The hope of America does not lie in political reform but in a sweeping revival of the American church.

I Pray for Missionaries and Pastors

"The harvest is truly plenteous, but the laborers are few; Pray ye therefore the Lord of the harvest, that he will send forth laborers into his harvest" (Mt. 9:37-38). I also pray for **missionaries** by name who have already been sent and those who God may be sending. I pray for specific needs that I know of. I ask God to help them grow deep in their theology and strong in their faith. I ask God to send someone along to encourage them with a kind word, a caring look, a listening ear, a gift, and if not, that they would learn how to encourage themselves with the joy of their salvation.

"Praying also for us, that God would open unto us a door of utterance, to speak the mystery of Christ, for which I am also in bonds; That I may make it manifest, as I ought to speak" (Col. 4:3-4). Paul asked the church in Colosse to pray for him that he would open his mouth boldly and make known the gospel as he ought to speak. I have a group of **pastors** that I pray for by name daily. Once again I mention specific needs I become aware of, but I always ask God to give them a clear and passionate vision of Christ and the gospel. I pray that God would give them unity of spirit among their congregation and a great harvest of souls for the glory of God and the good of the body. I pray God would bless their families and keep them morally pure. I pray they would endure opposition and make full proof of their ministry. I pray they would take seriously their call to the ministry. "Take heed to the ministry which thou hast received in the Lord, that thou fulfill it" (Col. 4:17). There are many good ministries that need prayer, put them in this category and remember them daily.

I Pray for Others

I pray for my **friends.** People I have grown to love through our mutual faith in Christ. Because of Christ there is a great capacity for friendship and prayer is a great enabler and sustainer. I pray for my **enemies;** those people God sends into our lives to strengthen our faith and purify our souls, those who oppose us because of the blessing of Christ in our lives. Expect enemies; accept them as part and parcel of the journey. Jesus had his share of them, why should we expect any different.

Praying categorically helps me stay on track. When the Holy Spirit has me pray about one thing that leads to another, I always know where to go back to. The categories are basically the same yet the prayers themselves are often different. I have found the Holy Spirit works very well in this structure.

I want to end this chapter with a caution. Structure is very good but too much structure can quench the work of God's spirit in prayer. You run the risk of mindless chanting or vain repetitions. Someone once said any truth taken to extreme soon becomes heresy. The prayers of this chapter are but suggested guidelines in helping to show the benefit of structure. It is not intended to be a formula that turns into mindless chanting or vain repetitions.

Chapter Three:

The Blessing of Private Prayer

The life of Christ was among many things, an example for us to follow. Jesus had a private prayer life. "And in the morning, rising up a great while before day, he went out, and departed into a solitary place, and there prayed" (Mk 1:35). It is recorded after the feeding of the five thousand that "straightway Jesus constrained his disciples to get into a boat and to go before him unto the other side, while he sent the multitudes away. And when he had sent the multitudes away, he went up into a mountain privately to pray; and when evening was come, he was there alone (Mt. 14:22-23).

Sermon Notes on Secret Praying

In what is known as the Sermon on the Mount, Jesus clearly teaches on private prayer. "And when thou prayest, thou shalt not be as the hypocrites are: for they love to pray standing in the synagogues and the corners of the streets, that they may be seen of men. Verily I say unto you, they have their reward. But thou, when thou prayest, enter into thy closet, and when thou hast shut the door, pray to thy Father who is in secret; and thy Father who seeth in secret shall reward thee openly."(Mt. 6:5-6) I've heard it said that if you really want to know who you are, get alone with God in prayer, for who you are when you are alone in prayer is who you are, and nothing more.

There is a place for all kinds of prayers. There is a place for public praying. Scripture records that Jesus prayed publicly. Before feeding the five thousand he asked the Father's blessing on the five loaves and two fishes. At the raising of Lazarus he stopped and publicly thanked God for hearing him. Jesus prayed with his disciples at the Passover meal just prior to going out to Gethsemane. I believe scripture encourages us to pray publicly. Pray before meals. Pray with your children before going to bed. Pray in the hospitals with those who are sick. We should pray in public but if a person's prayer life consists solely of public prayers, something is seriously wrong.

PETER'S PRIVATE PRAYER LIFE

In Acts 10 God was about to do a great thing. He was going to save a house full of gentiles in the home of a Roman soldier. He was going to use the reluctant apostle Peter to speak to them, but first he was going to speak to him during his private prayer time. Cornelius, the Roman soldier, had been praying himself. He prayed some good Jewish prayers, probably some Psalms and rabbicanal prayers he had learned at the synagogue he helped finance. He was devout and sincere, yet as lost as a goose in tall grass. God sent an angel to tell him to call for a man named Peter who was staying in the house of Simon. Simon was a tanner and lived in Joppa by the sea. At the same time the angel was speaking to Cornelius, Peter was in private prayer. It was at noon, one of the Jewish hours of prayer. Peter was up on the roof top and God gave him the vision of a great sheet filled with all kinds of unclean animals. These animals were ones the Jews were forbidden to eat. The Lord spoke to him and told him to kill and eat them. Peter refused but the Lord persisted. He repeated the message three times. Peter was perplexed at the vision and didn't know what it meant. He heard some voices downstairs inquiring about him and the Spirit told him to go with these men. The men told him about Cornelius, but Peter was struggling with his theology of salvation by grace. Could it be that God intended to save the gentiles and give them salvation by grace through faith? When Peter entered the home of Cornelius he made it clear that it was unlawful for him to keep company with gentiles. Somewhere between entering the home and the sermon he preached to the gentile household, Peter understood the vision God gave him during his prayer time. He understood, no man is common or unclean, so all men should be given the opportunity to hear the gospel and receive Christ by grace through faith alone. Peter preached the gospel and the Lord saved Cornelius and his household. In astonishment, Peter recognized the pouring out of the Holy Spirit on these gentile converts was just the same as it had been when the Holy Spirit was poured out on Jewish believers at Pentecost. Peter then baptized them and welcomed them into the church. This had a life changing effect on Peter and his faith. Private prayer is a good place to hear from God. Private prayer is where our personal faith becomes strong. "But ye beloved, building up yourselves on your most holy faith, praying in the Holy Spirit" (Jude 20). Private prayer may be one of the greatest evidences of a genuine and sincere faith.

Daniels Private Prayer Life

Much of the book of Daniel concerns the record of his prayer life, both public and private. In chapter two, God gave a dream to King Nebuchadnezzar then took the memory of that dream away. God troubled the king until he demanded his counselors tell him the dream and its meaning. He threatened to destroy them all if they did not do as he commanded. This was no idle threat and they all knew it. Daniel summoned his friends, Hananiah, Mishael, and Azariah to desire mercies from the God of heaven. They prayed God would reveal the dream and its meaning. When the secret was revealed to Daniel in a night vision, he blessed the God of heaven. Daniel told his friends, "Blessed be the name of God forever and ever; for wisdom and might are his. And he changeth the times and the seasons; he removeth kings, and setteth up kings: he giveth wisdom unto the wise, and knowledge to those who know understanding: He revealeth the deep and secret things; he knoweth what is in the darkness, and the light dwelleth with him. I thank thee, and praise thee, O thou God of my fathers, who hast given me wisdom and might, and hast made known unto me now what we desired of thee; for thou hast now made known unto us the king's matter" (Dan. 2:17-23). Daniel saw a vision of four world kingdoms, how they would rise and how they would someday end. That's no small revelation!

Daniel knew that there was a God in heaven who reveals secrets. He also knew the posture of prayer would be the best possible position for him to receive that revelation. I wonder how many secrets go unrevealed because of the lack of prayer. God knows the secrets to solving marriage problems, parenting problems, health problems, money problems, church problems, etc. "But as it is written, Eye hath not seen, no ear heard, neither have entered into the heart of man, the things which God hath prepared for them that love him. But God hath revealed them unto us by his Spirit: for the Spirit searcheth all things, yea, the deep things of God. For what man knoweth the things of a man, except the spirit of man which is in him? even so the things of God knoweth no man, but the Spirit of God. Now we have received, not the spirit of the world, but the

Spirit who is of God; that we might know the things that are freely given to us of God. Which things also we speak, not in words which man's wisdom teacheth, but which the Holy Spirit teacheth, comparing spiritual things with spiritual" (1 Cor. 2:9-13).

THE END OF THE AGES

Sometimes we receive revelations of things we're not even looking for. Daniel was in a special time of private prayer and fasting. He was confessing his sins and the sins of his fathers. "And while I was speaking and praying, and confessing my sin and the sin of my people Israel, and presenting my supplication before the Lord my God, for the holy mountain of my God; yea, while I was speaking in prayer, even the man Gabriel, whom I had seen in the vision at the beginning, being caused to fly swiftly, touched me about the time of the evening oblation. And he informed me, and talked with me, and said, O Daniel, I am now come forth to give thee skill and understanding" (Dan. 9:20-22). Daniel also heard of God's plan for the end of the ages. "And I heard, but I understood not: then said I, O my Lord, what shall be the end of these things? And he said, Go thy way, Daniel: for the words are closed up and sealed till the time of the end" (Dan. 12:8-9).

THE BLESSINGS OF THOSE
WHO PRAY IN SECRET

Psalms 91 is my favorite Psalm. I have often been encouraged as I have pondered over its truths. I approach this Psalm by seeing "the secret place of the Most High" as the secret place of prayer referred to by Jesus in Matthew 6:5-6. There are many blessing in this Psalm, especially for those who spend time dwelling in the secret place of prayer.

Verse 1 – He who dwelleth in the secret place of the Most High shall abide under of the shadow of the Almighty.

My dwelling place is a modest house in the state of Michigan. It is my home where I spend the majority of my days. It is where I have made many good memories with my wife and family. Private prayer is where we develop a sense of being at home with God, and make good memories. It's where we feel as close to him as if you were standing in his shadow. It is common knowledge that the safest place for a sheep is closest to the shepherd. I believe one of the greatest ways to draw near to God and have him draw near to you is in the private place of prayer.

Verse 2 – I will say of the Lord, He is **my** refuge and **my** fortress, **my** God: in him will I trust.

He is **a** refuge and fortress for many people, but oh the blessing when he becomes **my** refuge and fortress, **my** place of protection. "Except the Lord build the house, they labor in vain that build it; except the Lord keep the city, the watchman waketh but in vain" (Psa. 127:1). I can say with Jacob, "few and evil have the days of the years of my pilgrimage been" (Gen 47:9). Oh the Lord has been so good to me! Jacob had seen some hard days; Laban his father in law had deceived him in business, Esau his brother threatened to kill him and Joseph had been sold into slavery by his own brothers. Yet in the bigger picture of his life he could see that God had been good to him.

Verse 3 – Surely he shall deliver thee from the snare of the fowler, and from the noisome pestilence.

Private prayer allows us to be delivered from a lot of evil. We escape certain plots or schemes of the devil. "By which are given unto us exceeding great and precious promises: that by these ye might be partakers of the divine nature, having escaped the corruption that is in the world through lust" (2 Pet. 1:4). "There hath no temptation taken you but such as is common to man; but God is faithful, who will not permit you to be tempted above what you are able, but will with the temptation also make a way of escape, that ye may be able to bear it (1 Cor. 10:13). I love the line in the great old hymn "Sweet Hour of Prayer"- and oft escaped the tempters snare, by thy return sweet hour of prayer.

Verse 4 – He shall cover thee with his feathers, and under his wings shalt thou trust; his truth shall be thy shield and buckler.

An old mother hen will call her chicks to hide under her feathers when danger is near. Jesus knew this blessing of private prayer and longed for his people to know it. "O Jerusalem, Jerusalem, thou that killest the prophets, and stonest them who are sent unto thee, how often would I have gathered thy children together, even as a hen gathereth her chickens under her wings, and ye would not" (Mt. 23:37). How many prophets had spoken to the people of their need to humble themselves and pray, but they would not. They forfeited the blessing of God's tender care.

Verse 5 – Thou shalt not be afraid for the terror by night; nor for the arrow that flyeth by day.

"The wicked flee when no man pursueth: but the righteous are bold as a lion" (Prov. 28:1). His righteousness causes me to courageously say to fear, be gone, I have just spoken privately to the creator of the universe and everything is under control. "The Lord is my light and my salvation; whom shall I fear? The Lord is the strength of my life; of whom shall I be afraid? When the wicked, even mine enemies and my foes, came upon me to eat up my flesh, they stumbled and fell (Psa. 27:1-2).

Verse 6 - 8 - Nor for the pestilence that walketh in darkness; nor for the destruction that wasteth at noonday. A thousand shall fall at thy side, and ten thousand at thy right hand, but it shall not come nigh thee. Only with thine eyes shalt thou behold and see the reward of the wicked.

It seems that trouble can come any time of the day or night. The apostle Paul knew trouble. "We are troubled on every side, yet not distressed; perplexed, but not in despair; persecuted, but not forsaken; cast down, but not destroyed" (2 Cor. 4:8-9). In the world we are going to have tribulation, but be of good cheer, Jesus has overcome the world. Daily dwelling in the secret place of the most high is a glimpse of eternity. All the trouble of life is but one grain of sand on the vast seashore of eternity. Looking at life through the glasses of eternity makes sense out of all the trouble of this brief journey.

Verse 9-10 - Because thou hast made the Lord, who is my refuge, even the Most High thy habitation; there shall no evil befall thee, neither shall any plague come nigh thy dwelling.

Oh the peace and protection that comes from being at home in the secret place of prayer.

Verse 11-12 - For he shall give his angels charge over thee, to keep thee in all thy ways. They shall bear thee up in their hands, lest thou dash thy foot against a stone.

Satan quoted these verses to Jesus during his wilderness temptations. Though Satan knew well of Jesus' prayer life he didn't miss an opportunity to cast doubt on the promised blessings of those who pray privately. "For all the promises of God in him are yea, and in him Amen, unto the glory of God by us" (2 Cor. 1:20).

Verse 13 - Thou shalt tread upon the lion and the adder; the young lion and the dragon shalt thou trample under feet.

The lion and the serpent are figurative language for the devil. Satan opposes those who would follow Christ. He hinders us in our journey, and tempts us along life's way. Paul says in Ephesians 6 that after we have put on the whole armor of God we are to take our stand. Private prayer is where we give Satan his worst thrashing. Its here he senses his greatest resistance and flees while he still has a foot to hobble on. We are no match for Satan, but Satan is no match for Christ. Satan would certainly devour us in all our fleshly efforts to resist him, but prayer is spiritual business and he flees when the saint takes his stand in prayer. All good soldiers put the boots to Satan through the ministry of private prayer.

Verse 14 – Because he hath set his love upon me, therefore will I deliver him; I will set him on high, because he hath known my name.

"And the seventy returned again with joy, saying, Lord, even the demons are subject unto us through thy name" (Lu. 10:17). "Wherefore God hath also highly exalted him, and given him a name which is above every name: that at the name of Jesus every knee should bow, of things in heaven, and things in earth, and things under the earth; and that every tongue should confess that Jesus Christ is Lord, to the glory of God the Father" (Phil. 2:9-11). Scripture records over one thousand names, titles and attributes of him who is Lord of all, and yet the name of Jesus is at the top of the list. Oh what joy to know that name and what significance it holds throughout the whole of creation, that worthy name by which we are called.

Verse 15 – He shall call upon me, and I will answer him: I will be with him in trouble; I will deliver him, and honor him.

I hate to be alone in trouble. Things always seem worse when you feel alone. What a comfort just to know someone is there. Private prayer keeps me conscious of the truth that He is always there, and a very present help in time of trouble. I've come to the place that I would rather be in a rough sea with Jesus than a calm one without him. That's a perspective the world knows nothing of.

Verse 16 – With long life will I satisfy him, and show him my salvation.

Long life can't always be interpreted as many years. Some people live many years and when they die, very few people even know if they were ever here. Some people live a short life and are remembered a long time. In other words, some people live a long time after they are dead. They do something for God in a short life, while others do nothing for God in a long life. When a person sees salvation, really sees the salvation of the Lord, his goodness and mercy, his love and grace; his life changes because he is satisfied with God alone. He has meaning and purpose that will guide him throughout the rest of his life. Eternal living is a long life. Oh the blessing of private prayer.

Chapter Four:

Power in Prayer

I had been speaking at a conference and was asked to join a panel for a question and answer time. I agreed even though I am not always comfortable with Q & A times. Several years previously after a Q & A time I came back sat with my wife and asked her how I did. She said that I had given great answers; unfortunately, my answers didn't have much to do with the questions. So, since then, I've always been a little nervous. I think the eleven years I spent as a Michigan State Trooper may also have had something to do with my uneasiness. I would be distracted trying to figure out motives instead of really listening to the questions. None the less, there I was on a question panel when a couple said they prayed for their children but their prayers seemed to lack power. They asked if I had any suggestions on what to do. I hadn't planned this answer but I think it is a good one. I said, find something powerful and pray it. I then went on to explain how to pray the scriptures.

Praying the Scriptures

Three verses quickly came to mind. "For the word of God is living, and **powerful,** and sharper than any two-edged sword, piercing even to the dividing asunder of soul and spirit, and of the joints and marrow, and is a discerner of the thoughts and intents of the heart" (Heb. 4:12). Secondly, Jesus said in answer to the Sadducees, "Do ye not therefore err, because ye know not the scriptures, neither the **power** of God?" (Mk 12:24). And finally "Through faith we understand that the worlds were framed by the word of God..." (Heb. 11:3). There are many scriptural metaphors to describe the word of God. These indicate some of how the Word functions when spoken in prayer.

The Word of God is Like Milk

"As newborn babes, desire the sincere milk of the word that ye may grow by it" (1 Pet. 2:2).

When my mother passed away at the age of 49, I asked my father for her Bible. My mother was a praying woman and in the back of her Bible she had written a prayer for me. She prayed, "Oh God that my son would fall in love with your word". My mother had wisdom enough to know that if I fell in love with the word of God many other worries she had for me would take care of themselves. Now, I had flunked the fifth grade because I couldn't read. I had dyslexia and didn't find much success in reading until my junior year of college. But nevertheless, her prayers were answered. Now I love to read, especially my Bible. It was a powerful prayer because it was according to scripture. "O how love I thy law! It is my meditation all the day" (Psa. 119:97). "Great peace have they who love thy law: and nothing shall offend them" (Psa. 119:165). I have found that most parents want their children to love the word of God, but few pray that they would.

BREAD

"It is written; Man shall not live by bread alone, but by every word that proceedeth out of the mouth of God" (Mt. 4:4).

Bread is a staple food throughout much of the world. It is served in one form or another at least once a day in many homes. Jesus encouraged people to pray after a certain manner, "Give us this day our daily bread" (Mt. 6:11). Just as bread nourishes our physical body, so does the word of God nourish and strengthen our spirit. If a man wants to be strong physically he must eat physical food. If a man wants to be strong spiritually he must eat spiritual food. The prophet Jeremiah said "Thy words were found and I did eat them, and thy word was unto me the joy and rejoicing of mine heart; for I am called by thy name, O Lord God of hosts" (Jer. 15:16).

SWORD

"And take the helmet of salvation, and the sword of the Spirit, which is the word of God" (Eph. 6:17).

At the time this scripture was written, the weapon of choice for hand to hand combat was the Roman Sword. It was usually sixteen to eighteen inches long and double edged, enabling the soldier to cut down his enemies regardless of which way he swung it. It was also made of heavy enough steel to be used for piercing. "For the word of God is living and powerful, sharper than any two-edged sword, piercing even to the dividing asunder of soul and spirit, and of the joints and marrow, and is a discerner of the thoughts and intents of the heart" (Heb. 4:12). When the Christian soldier stands in complete armor according to Ephesians 6:12-18, and takes hold of the sword of the spirit with the powerful hand of prayer, he puts to flight the devil and his host of wicked spirits. "Submit yourselves therefore to God. Resist the devil and he will flee from you" (Jas.4:7).

LAMP AND A LIGHT

"Thy word is a lamp unto my feet and a light unto my path" (Psa. 199:105).

Every man with 20/20 vision is rendered blind when he is in abject darkness. In other words, perfect eyes aren't any better than a blind man's without light. It's like a blind man leading a blind man and both of them falling into a ditch because neither can see. Light is the secret to seeing, and probably why it was the first thing God created. "The entrance of thy words giveth light; it giveth understanding to the simple" (Psa. 119:130). Apart from the word of God we have no sure understanding of the will of God. "And this is the confidence that we have in him, that if we ask anything according to his will, he heareth us; and if we know that he hear us, whatever we ask, we know that we have the petitions that we desired of him" (1 John 5:14-15). The better we know scripture the better we know how to pray.

WATER

"Husbands, love your wives, even as Christ also loved the church, and gave himself for it; that he might sanctify and cleanse it with the washing of water by the word" (Eph. 5:25-26).

When a husband loves his wife according to the word and desires to make fellowship the highest priority (Phil 2:1-4) it will have a cleansing effect on both of them. The truth of God's word will pour over the couple giving them the wisdom and grace to live in oneness. Sin has always been the culprit that brings separation and condemnation. The word tells us that Christ came and condemned sin, Romans 8:2. "If we confess our sins, he is faithful and just to forgive us our sins, and to cleanse us from all unrighteousness" (I John 1:9). When couples employ the principals of this truth, a necessary washing of the water takes place in their relationship. Once again, praying scripture is powerful.

FIRE AND A HAMMER

"Is not my word like as a fire? saith the Lord; and like a hammer that breaketh the rock in pieces?" (Jer. 23:29).

You may be asking, how you pray the scriptures like a hammer, and what kind of rock it breaks. First of all, the word is a rock smashing hammer. It's not a tack hammer, but a sledge hammer. The rock is symbolic of a stronghold. Strongholds were not made of straw or wood but of stone or brick and mortar. "For though we walk in the flesh, we do not war after the flesh: For the weapons of our warfare are not carnal, but mighty through God to the pulling down of strongholds" (2 Cor. 10:3-4).

If you are going to break up and remove a large piece of cement you use a sledge hammer. The first time you swing it, you may only leave a powder mark. You swing again and again until you see a stress crack, then you pour it on until the first chunk is broken off and taken away. The first piece is usually the most difficult to remove, but when it is, the whole is weakened. It begins to shatter more and more easily until it can be completely eliminated.

Let's say you have a child you have brought up in the ways of the Lord. Let's say they know right from wrong yet they are in a pattern of choosing the wrong. When you talk with them about it they say they don't know why they choose wrong, they knew better. You may want to include this scripture in your daily prayer. "And this I pray, that your love may abound yet more and more in knowledge and in all judgment" (Phil. 1:9). Don't just pray that they would know right from wrong but that they would make the right judgments. A wrong judgment takes all the right knowledge and throws it to the wind. So often, in the midst of a choice to do right, there is a moment where we are tempted to compromise. It is at that time when prayer releases the powerful influence of the Holy Spirit to make the right choice.

This is a simple truth but I will say it anyway; the more we chose right the easier it becomes, the more we chose wrong, the easier it becomes. God gives us the liberty to make whatever choices we want, but he does not give us the liberty to choose the consequences. We live with the consequences. We reap what we sow and we live with what's in the barn. Our decisions affect our destiny. We need power from God in making the right decisions. Paul said that whenever he prayed for the Philippian church, he prayed for their love to abound more and more (Phil. 1:4). Let's say you pray this scripture once a week for your wayward child. In one year you will have prayed 52 times. That's a lot of pounding. Let's say you pray this scripture once a day for a year, that's 365 hits with the sledge hammer. Most strongholds will be broken down. Even the strongest of them will show significant weakening.

I need to say something here on perseverance. Certain kinds of praying are work. Hammering down strongholds is work. "…men ought always to pray and not to faint" (Lk. 18:1). "Epaphras, who is one of you, a servant of Christ, greeteth you, always laboring fervently for you in prayers, that you may stand perfect and complete in all the will of God" (Col. 4:12). Becoming strong in prayer on behalf of others, (intercessions) may be unseen by man but it does not go unnoticed by God. It may appear that things get worse when you start hammering away in prayer. Expect some discouragement, do you think the enemy is going to run at the first sight of battle. "If thou faint in the day of adversity, thy strength is small" (Prov. 24:10).Our faith is greatly strengthened in the school of enduring prayer.

PERSEVERING IN PRAYER

"Praying always with all prayer and supplication in the Spirit, and watching thereunto with all perseverance and supplications for all saints" (Eph. 6:18). "Rejoicing in hope; patient in tribulation; continuing diligently in prayer" (Rom. 12:12). "Continue in prayer, and watch in the same with thanksgiving" (Col. 4:2). It is hard to persevere or continue diligently in something you haven't begun. Someone you love may be struggling, take them on in prayer and persevere. "Bear ye one another's burdens, and so fulfill the law of Christ" (Gal. 6:2). "Ask and it shall be given you; seek, and ye shall find; knock, and it shall be opened unto you; for everyone that asketh receiveth; and he that seeketh findeth; and to him that knocketh it shall be opened. Or what man is there of you, whom, if his son asks bread, will he give him a stone? Or if he asks a fish, will he give him a serpent? If ye then, being evil, know how to give good gifts unto your children, how much more shall your Father in heaven give good things to them that ask him?" (Mt. 7:7-11). Jesus spoke of a widow who asked a judge to avenge her of her adversary. He wouldn't hear her case for awhile but eventually her persistence won out. "And shall not God avenge his own elect, who cry day and night unto him, though he bear long with them? I tell you that he will avenge them speedily" (Lk. 18:7-8). Saints of old used to have an expression for persevering prayer; it was called "praying through". Take on a burden for someone, or for your own soul. Make it a matter of daily prayer. Find a powerful scriptural prayer and pray it through.

I LOVE TO SPLIT WOOD

We have heated our house with wood for over thirty years. I love to get on my jeans and old flannel shirt, throw my saws and maul in the back of the truck and head for the woods. My favorite wood to split is straight grained oak or ash. One swing and they just bust apart. But not all wood is so easy to split. Sometimes it's so full of knots and forks you know from the start that it's going to take more than one or two swings. You come down with your monster maul and it bounces back up with kind of a resisting sound, known only to those who have done this sort of work. You get ready for the challenge. You swing again and again, trying to hit the same place and not make a new mark each time. Your determination to win increases and eventually you hear the sound of the wood weakening and it pops apart. You knew when you started it was going to be a hard one, but perseverance paid off.

"Elijah was a man subject to like passions as we are, and he prayed earnestly that it might not rain: and it rained not on the earth for the space of three years and six months. And he prayed again, and the heaven gave rain, and the earth brought forth her fruit" (Jas. 5:17-18). James only records that Elijah prayed earnestly. However in 1 Kings 18, we read 'how' he prayed earnestly. After God had heard Elijah's prayer and fire came down and consumed the sacrifice along with the altar, he went to the top of Mt. Carmel and put his face between his knees and began to pray for rain. "And said to his servant, Go up now, look toward the sea. And he went up, and looked, and said, there is nothing. And he said, Go again seven times. And it came to pass at the seventh time, that he said, Behold, there ariseth a little cloud out of the sea, like a man's hand. And he said, Go up, and say unto Ahab, Prepare thy chariot, and get thee down, that the rain stop thee not. And it came to pass in the meanwhile, that the heaven was black with clouds and wind, and there was a great rain" (1 Ki. 18:43-45). "And let us not be weary in well doing: for in due season we shall reap, if we faint not" (Gal. 6:9).

Genesis 32 records that Jacob wrestled with the angel of the Lord. As the day was beginning to break the angel said, let me go for the dawn is approaching. Jacob said he would not let him go until he blessed him. As a result Jacob was blessed with a new name, Israel, which carries with it the meaning of a man who wrestled with God and prevailed. We know that no man wrestles with God and prevails unless God in his sovereign grace ordains it. Somewhere in the great mystery of prayer there is a place for this kind of praying and a blessing for those whose hearts are determined to struggle through.

Learn Some Scriptural Prayers

Find out what the apostles and the prophets prayed. Scripture is full of their prayers and the powerful results of them. Here is but a short list of great scriptural prayers that would be good to memorize and incorporate in your own prayers.

"For this cause we also, since the day we heard it, <u>do not cease to pray for you,</u> and to desire that ye might be filled with the knowledge of his will in all wisdom and spiritual understanding; That ye might walk worthy of the Lord unto all pleasing, being fruitful in every good work, and increasing in the knowledge of God; Strengthened with all might, according to his glorious power, unto all patience and longsuffering with joyfulness; Giving thanks unto the Father, who hath made us fit to be partakers of the inheritance of the saints in light: Who hath delivered us from the power of darkness, and hath translated us into the kingdom of his dear Son: In whom we have redemption through his blood, even the forgiveness of sins" (Col. 1:9-14).

"For this cause I bow my knees unto the Father of our Lord Jesus Christ, of whom the whole family in heaven and earth is named, that he would grant you, according to the riches of his glory, to be strengthened with might by his Spirit in the inner man; That Christ may dwell in your hearts by faith; that ye, being rooted and grounded in love, May be able to comprehend with all saints what is the breadth, and length, and depth, and height; and to know the love of Christ which passeth knowledge, that ye might be filled with all the fullness of God. Now unto him who is able to do exceedingly abundantly above all we ask or think, according to the power that worketh in us, unto him be glory in the church by Christ Jesus throughout all ages, world without end. Amen" (Eph. 3:14-21).

"That the God of our Lord Jesus Christ, the Father of glory, may give unto you the spirit of wisdom and revelation in the knowledge of him: the eyes of your understanding being enlightened; that ye may know what is the hope of his calling, and what is the riches of the glory of his inheritance in the saints, and what is the exceeding greatness of his power toward us who believe, according to the working of his mighty power," (Eph. 1:17-19).

"I thank my God upon every remembrance of you, always in every prayer of mine for you all making request with joy,

"And this I pray, that your love may abound yet more and more in knowledge and in all judgment; that ye may approve things that are excellent; that ye may be sincere and without offence till the day of Christ, being filled with the fruits of righteousness, which are by Jesus Christ, unto the glory and praise of God" (Phil. 1:3-4, 9-11).

I pray that all my children shall be taught of the Lord and great shall be the peace of my children. I pray that they shall be established in righteousness and kept far from oppression, and that fear and terror would be kept far from them. I pray that no weapon formed against them would ever prosper and that every tongue that rises up against them in judgment God would condemn, for this is the heritage of the servants of the Lord, and their righteousness is from me saith the Lord. This is a paraphrase of Isaiah 54:13-14, 17.

There is power in the scriptures and there is power in praying the scriptures. When you add perseverance, you have learned a great lesson in the school of prayer.

"For God is my witness, whom I serve with my spirit in the gospel of his Son that without ceasing I make mention of you always in my prayers" (Rom. 1:9).

Chapter Five:

Preventative Prayer

Most people would agree that an ounce of prevention is worth a pound of cure. Why suffer certain health problems when a simple change in diet and exercise could have prevented it. If something as simple as washing our hands and taking vitamin C will increase our chance of avoiding a cold, then it's worth doing. We are going to be exposed to germs, its part of life, but if we can do something to prevent their effect on us, then it's wise to do so.

The prince of this world, Satan, loves to take advantage when our resistance is down. Sometimes the fatigue of ministry lowers our resistance against him. I used to think that being busy in the ministry was all I needed to keep him away. The simple truth is, those nearest the front lines, can expect the greatest opposition. Understanding and employing preventative prayer has been a great help in our journey of faith. I think it is valuable to all believers and especially those committed to ministry.

EARLY IN OUR MINISTRY

Five years after committing my life to Christ, I sensed God's call to preach. My wife confirmed that call and within days I had resigned my job of eleven years. Our bank account grew poor but our marriage and family grew rich in the things that money can't buy. It was during those early days that I established my family as my main ministry. My preaching would be an overflow from it. I didn't want to stand in the pulpit and tell others about the power of Christ to transform lives without it being true in my own home. You may have a different philosophy of ministry, but after 25 years, this one has proven itself to me. "Prove all things; hold fast that which is good" (1 Thess. 5:21). "But watch thou in all things, endure afflictions, do the work of an evangelist, make full proof of thy ministry" (2 Tim.4:5). A sound marriage and strong family are the best credentials you can have for a preaching ministry. They are also scriptural. See 1 Timothy 3 and Titus 1.

The first few years of ministry were extremely busy. There were so many changes in our life. I was pastor of a small church. I was attending Bible school and working a part time job. We had decided to home school our children. We were having home Bible studies with new believers. My wife made our home a place given to hospitality. It is no small task to juggle the balance between a solace for your family and the ministry of hospitality to others.

She truly was, and is, a master of both. Even with such an amazing woman by my side the days were filled with activity.

Church

The church was thirty miles from home, so Joyce would often take food and we would stay all day at the church. Often we shared the day with visitors. It was a joy to get to know them, but by the end of the day I looked forward to being alone with my dear wife and children. I would turn off the lights and lock the building. Ahh, we were finally in the car and headed home. Sometimes, before we had even made it out of the driveway, something would happen and chaos would break out. Attitudes were instantly non-Christian, especially the pastor's. It didn't happen every time, but it happened often enough for me to question, "Why?"

Vacation

Things like this would happen at other times as well. We would be planning a camping vacation. We loved being together and looked forward to these special times. Joyce is a master at planning and building anticipation for our family time together. Things would be going well, then, ten minutes before leaving, something would happen, something would break, something would be lost, etc. Chaos would break out, attitudes would sour, and we would leave feeling like we had just been robbed. We would ask forgiveness and make it right, but there would still seem to be a cloud hanging over us. Why?

MINISTRY

We would preach at week long camps in the summer. All week I would be preaching and ministering to people. By the end I just wanted to be with my wife and kids. Physically, we had been together, but all too often my mind was on my messages. As we left the camp, or maybe when we got home, something would happen that would steal the joy we normally had. Things seemed so out of proportion. Misdemeanors were turned into federal cases. It would happen so quickly, so unexpectedly. Events that hardly warranted a response seemed like a catastrophe. It didn't happen every time but it happened often enough for me to ask the question, "Why?"

TRAVEL

I love to be home and I love to be with my family. When I have to travel alone, I hardly get out of sight before I start thinking about returning home. In 2 Corinthians 11 Paul gives a list of the sacrifices he made in serving Christ. I could only marginally identify with one, "in journeyings often". Only God knows my heart and only He determines what an acceptable sacrifice is. With that said, you would think all would be bliss to get back home. Most of the time it was bliss, but there were other times when something would happen. Our desired good reunion would go up in smoke. Once again I would ask, "Why?" I knew the danger of my family hearing me preach one thing and live another. I knew they would believe what they saw more than what they heard. But even so, these things happened more than I would have liked. "Why?"

The Enemy of My Soul

In those early days I knew almost nothing about spiritual warfare, but the Lord was beginning to give me some insight to my "why" questions. John 10:10 says, "The thief cometh not, but for to steal, and to kill, and to destroy." That verse described perfectly how I felt after one of these events. I felt as though I had been robbed. I felt as though so much of what I was trying to build up had been destroyed. Could it be the enemy of my soul was taking advantage of these situations? Was it possible for the devil to have any influence of this sort in my life? I became cautious over the next few months, with a sincere heart to find an answer. I found a scripture that seemed to lend some insight into my question, Luke 8:22-25.

THE STORMS

There are three types of storms in scripture. One is recorded in the book of Jonah. In chapter one verse two, God commands Jonah to go to Nineveh and preach. Verse three Jonah decides to go on a cruise instead. Verse four, God sends the storm and there is no calm until he is heading in the right direction. This storm is representative of the flesh.

A second type of storm is seen in Acts 27 when the apostle Paul is on a boat headed toward Rome. He is sailing with a group of sailors, soldiers, and fellow prisoners. It's storm season on the Mediterranean Sea. Paul gives them good counsel and a warning from the Lord. The captain, however, chooses to ignore his advice and everybody on the boat suffers the consequences. Some storms we experience are just because we are citizens of earth and in the world we are going to have tribulations. This storm is representative of the world.

This third type of storm I was reading about is found in the gospels, Matthew 8:23-27, Mark 4:35-41, and Luke 8:22-25. Jesus told his disciples to get into the boat. They were going to the other side. As they sailed, Jesus being tired from a full day of ministry, fell asleep. A storm came up on the lake quite suddenly. Now Peter and several of the other disciples were veteran seaman. They made their living fishing on the Sea of Galilee. This was no ordinary storm and they knew it. They panicked and woke Jesus accusing him of not caring for them. Jesus arose, rebuked the storm, and afterwards addressed their theology. If the storm had been sent by God, Jesus would never have rebuked it. This storm was sent by the enemy, and so, is representative of the devil.

The following thoughts stood out to me. The storm apparently came up quite suddenly and created chaos. The storm also caused them to lose faith. Did he not say they were going to the other side? In the middle of this storm, they accused Jesus of his lack of care. This seemed to describe my situation more than I wanted to admit.

A Plan

To be forewarned is to be forearmed. Luke 22:31-32 held the answer to my "why" questions. "Simon, Simon, behold, Satan hath desired to have you that he may sift you as wheat; but I have prayed for thee, that thy faith fail not." Jesus didn't say he was praying for Peter, (present tense). He didn't say he was going to pray for him, (future tense). He said he had already prayed for him, (past tense). Peter was moments away from denying Christ and going through the roughest three days of his life. Jesus knew it and prayed one thing for him. He prayed his faith would not fail, like it had during the storm. Jesus knew that the shield of faith would quench all the fiery darts of the wicked one.

I decided to run an experiment. Why build a boat without pushing it out in the water to see if it floats? Why develop a theology without an exercise of faith? I decided to pray in advance of things, and see what happened. I began to pray against the enemy on my way home. I made certain crossroads my reminders to pray. I prayed before ministries began that Satan would be denied any permission to harass me or my family. I asked the Lord to go before me and scatter the plans of the enemy. I prayed every evil desire Satan had would backfire on him a thousand fold. I would accept everything God had for me but I would reject anything Satan had for me. Within three months the change was noticeable. I told my family what I had been doing and they joined me in preventative prayer. We have found that praying preventively is more powerful than praying while you're in a mess, (present tense). It is also more powerful than trying to pray your way out of a mess, (past tense). Cleaning up is never easy.

Over the years this kind of praying has expanded into many areas of our life. We know from experience that anything special needs preventative prayer. If you are planning a family reunion, bathe it in preventative prayer. Holidays such as Christmas, Easter, Thanksgiving, birthdays, anniversaries, you can include everything from romance to business ventures. "Be anxious for nothing; but in every thing by prayer and supplication with thanksgiving let your request be made known unto God" (Phil. 4:6).

One of the great expressions of our faith is to pray believing that God hears and cares for us. "But without faith it is impossible to please him; for he that cometh to God must believe that he is, and that he is a rewarder of them that diligently seek him" (Heb. 11:6).

CHAPTER SIX:

PRAYERS THAT SANCTIFY

I believe the Bible teaches that "all have sinned, and come short of the glory of God" (Rom. 3:23). I believe "sin is the transgression of the law" (1 John 3:4). The law of God demands perfection and one violation of that law makes me as guilty as if I had broken all the laws of God, (Jas. 2:10). I was born without any hope of ever doing enough good to make it to heaven. I could never be good enough to be right with God. In other words I was condemned from birth because of the first man, Adam, and his sin, (Rom. 5:12, 18). How could I a sinful man ever make myself right with a holy God? The answer is simple. I CAN'T! I need a savior, and God has provided only one, "And this is life eternal, that they might know thee, the only true God, and Jesus Christ, whom thou hast sent" (John 17:3). This savior is God's son. His name is Jesus. He justified me and redeemed me from the curse of the law, (Rom. 3:24, Gal. 3:13). So that I with all those who are justified, would declare God's righteousness, knowing that "God is just and the justifier of him which believes in Jesus" (Rom. 3:26). Being right with God is not something we do; it is something God has done and by his grace declares us to be. "Therefore being justified by faith, we have peace with God though our Lord Jesus Christ" (Rom. 5:1). This is the gospel message.

A Prayer that Justifies

Luke 18 records a parable where Jesus illustrates the gospel. Two men went up to the temple to pray. The one was a very religious man. In his prayer he stated that he was a good man recounting his religious activity. He thought he was just and right before God because of his good works. He thought he was better than other men, who, in his sight, were sinners. He had good breeding and blood lines. He had formal religious training. He trusted in his efforts and condemned others who didn't measure up to his standards.

The other man was a crook and a traitor to his country. Money had played too big a part in his life. He gave into the vices that so often accompany greedy people. He knew he would have no place in heaven because of his sin. So when he prayed, he made a cry for mercy. Luke 18:13 records his prayer, "Lord, be merciful to me a sinner". He was so humbled by the consciousness of his sinful condition he couldn't even lift up his eyes toward heaven. His hand clinched into a fist, he struck his chest and he prayed the sinner's prayer. Verse 14 records God's response, "I tell you this man went down to his house justified rather than the other; for every one that exalteth himself shall be abased; and he that humbleth himself shall be exalted."

The Bible emphasizes this truth from Genesis to Revelation. It is the only true gospel. When a person comes to the knowledge of his helpless and hopeless sinful condition under the law, and ceases trying to work his way to heaven by his own goodness, he can pray the sinner's prayer for mercy. God will justify him. "But to him that worketh not, but believeth on him that justifieth the ungodly, his faith is counted for righteousness" (Rom. 4:5). "Not by works of righteousness which we have done, but according to his mercy he saved us…" (Titus 3:5). All other prayers stand in the shadow of the one prayer that justifies. "Lord, be merciful to me a sinner".

PRAYERS THAT SANCTIFY

We are recipients of justification and recipients only. Sanctification, however, is something we are participants in. Sanctification is not earning our identity in Christ, but bringing our behavior in line with our identity. It's growing in the grace and knowledge of our Lord and Savior Jesus Christ, (2 Pet. 3:18). If I live to be a hundred, I will never be anymore justified than I was the moment I first believed, but as I grow older I will become more sanctified. Prayer is indispensable in sanctification. I would like to share three prayers I have learned that help in this process.

A Prayer for Wisdom

Wisdom is the proper application of knowledge and understanding. Many times we know the clinical information of a given situation. That is to say, we have knowledge of the facts. Often times we understand why things are the way they are, yet, we lack the wisdom to choose the best course. This is an excellent time to pray. "If any of you lack wisdom, let him ask it of God, that giveth to all men liberally, and upbraideth not; and it shall be given him" (Jas. 1:5).

There are two kinds of wisdom which are readily identified. One is from above and the other is from below. "If ye have bitter envying and strife in your hearts, glory not, and lie not against the truth. This wisdom descendeth not from above, but is earthly, sensual, and devilish. For where envying and strife are, there is confusion and every evil work. But the wisdom that is from above is first pure, then peaceable, gentle, and easy to be entreated, full of mercy and good fruits, without partiality, and without hypocrisy" (Jas. 3:14-17).

Wisdom, however, is not enough. Solomon was acknowledged as one of the wisest men who ever lived, yet, he died a babbling old fool, worshiping idols in the temples of his foreign wives, and God was not pleased with him. See 1 Kings 11:4-10. People traveled "from the uttermost parts of the earth to hear the wisdom of Solomon; and, behold, a greater than Solomon is here" (Matt 12:42). Wisdom needs help. I can know what wisdom would have me to do, yet, lack the power to do it.

A Prayer for Grace

"Let us therefore come boldly unto the throne of grace that we may obtain mercy, and find grace to help in time of need" (Heb. 4:16). Grace is the divine enabling power of God that helps us do what wisdom teaches us we should do. "And God is able to make all grace abound toward you; that you, always having all sufficiency in all things, may abound to every good work" (2 Cor. 9:8). Many times we hear the wisdom of God. We know the right thing to do, but don't do it. Our spirit is willing but our flesh is weak. This is when we exchange the wisdom of God for the wisdom of man. "Let no man deceive himself. If any man among you seemeth to be wise in this world, let him become a fool, that he may be wise. For the wisdom of this world is foolishness with God. For it is written, He taketh the wise in their own craftiness. And again, The Lord knoweth the thoughts of the wise, that they are vain" (1 Cor 3:18-20).

A RECENT EXAMPLE

We had just come home from a busy week of travel and ministry. It was so good to be home and I had many things planned for the week. I got up early, had my prayer time, ran and exercised. Joyce made oatmeal and we sat down for breakfast. I began making my list of things I wanted to do for the day.

- #1. Work on messages - the importance of God's word in our daily life.
- #2. Work on Prayer book (the one you are now reading)
- #3. Work on Scripture memory
- #4. Fix the tail lights on the car (I dread this but I had to do it)
- #5. Stack wood on the back porch (a job I enjoy doing)
- #6. Return phone calls
- #7. Correspondence (there were two letters I wanted to write)

I knew this is a dangerous time for me. I knew I had more things on my list than is humanly possible to accomplish in one day. I knew I was setting myself up for feeling overwhelmed. When I feel overwhelmed I can easily become driven. When driven I tend to be picky and try to steer others at the same driven pace. This has happened to me before and I know what to do. Wisdom speaks to me, telling me to submit my schedule to the Lord and ask for grace. But instead I listened to the other wisdom, that voice speaking to me from deep within the dim regions of my darkened heart. That voice is followed by shouts of amen from the pit of hell. To some extent, the sin that's in me enjoys these moments of darkness, (John 3:19). I know what to do, but I'm just not doing it. As we continue to eat our oatmeal, it gets worse.

Joyce always does our income taxes. She had three months before they had to be done. But when you are driven it feels like everything needs to be done today. I asked her is she had them done yet. She said no but that she would finish them. Later in the morning, she was going to be watching three of the grandchildren... I asked her if she was going to be able to keep them quiet while I studied. (She is a proven master of caring for children.) She said she would play with them in the back room farthest from my study. A few bites of oatmeal later I asked her if she had transferred the information from our old atlas to the new one. There was no urgent need, but you never can tell when you might go on a sudden trip, right? She knows me, and knows what is happening to me. She smiles, gets out of her chair and comes over to me. She puts her arms around my head, pulls me to her and preaches a 45 minute sermon in a three second prayer. She prayed, "Oh God, help Tom to throw out the anchors and pray for daylight." Instantly, the Lord brought me out of a horrible pit, which I had dug, out of the miry clay. He set my feet on a rock and established my goings. I laughed as God's mercy and grace swept over me. I hugged my dear wife and asked her whatever made her pray that prayer. It was from a sermon I had preached about ten years ago. She said she had just read Acts 27:29 in her morning devotions and remembered the sermon. She spoke with wisdom from above. She was empowered by God's grace to help me in my time of need. I could have prayed for grace myself, many times I do, but this time I didn't. I thank God he joined us together as one.

JESUS HAD WISDOM AND GRACE

"And the child grew, and became strong in spirit, filled with wisdom; and the grace of God was upon him..." (Luke 2:40). And Jesus increased in wisdom and stature, and in favor with God and man" (Luke 2: 52). "And the Word was made flesh, and dwelt among us, and we beheld his glory, the glory as of the only begotten of the Father, full of grace and truth" (John 1:14). The last verse in the Bible says, "The grace of our Lord Jesus Christ be with you all. Amen" (Rev. 22:21). "But he giveth more grace, wherefore he saith, God resisteth the proud, but giveth grace unto the humble" (Jas. 4:6). A prayer for grace in the time of need is the humble acknowledgement of our dependence on God for power to do the right things. God has designed it that way so he gets all the glory and we get all the good.

When you know what to do and yet lack the power to do it, remember, ask God for the power of his grace. Jesus said to the apostle Paul, "My grace is sufficient for thee: for my strength is made perfect in weakness" (2 Cor. 12:9). Paul's response to God's grace was, "But by the grace of God I am what I am: and his grace which was given unto me was not in vain; but I labored more abundantly than they all: yet not I, but the grace of God which was with me" (1 Cor. 15:10). Is it any wonder that the apostle Paul began and ended all of his letters with grace?

Everything we do requires the divine enabling power of his grace. When you know God's grace is being given to you to do right, don't resist it or fail to walk in it. "Looking diligently lest any man fail of the grace of God; lest any root of bitterness springing up trouble you, and by it many be defiled" (Heb 12:15). Walking in grace is not easy, but it is something you can become strong in. "Thou therefore, my son, be strong in the grace that is in Christ Jesus" (2 Tim. 2:1). Yet wisdom would give a caution to those who are walking strong in the grace that is in Christ Jesus. Pray a prayer for protection from the evil one.

A Prayer for Protection from the Evil One

There is no prayer I pray more than for the Lord to keep me from the evil one. Jesus encouraged his disciples to pray, "lead us not into temptation but deliver us from the evil one" (Mt. 6:13, Lu. 11:4). When Jesus prayed for his disciples he prayed that the Father would not take them out of the world but that he would keep them from the evil one, (John 17:15). We may hear the wisdom of God with the grace of God upon us, yet, we are not immune to satanic attack. Sometimes, God, in his sovereignty, allows the enemy to assault his people, as in the case of Job. The old serpent, called the devil and Satan, is still more subtle than any beast of the field which the Lord God created, (Genesis 3:1). Peter cautioned us saying, "Be sober, be vigilant; because your adversary the devil, as a roaring lion, walketh about, seeking whom he may devour; Whom resist steadfast in the faith, knowing the same afflictions are accomplished in your brethren that are in the world" (1 Pet. 5:8-9). I am no match for Satan, but he is no match for Christ. I daily pray for the Lord to deny Satan any permission to assault me or my family in any way. Any evil desire the enemy has against me I pray the Lord turn it back upon his own wicked head a thousand fold. I daily ask the Lord to go before me and scatter the plans of the enemy and deliver me from his evil schemes.

These prayers have been a significant part of my life for the past twenty years. Only eternity will know the full extent they have played in my journey of faith. The apostle Paul said, "Prove all things; hold fast that which is good" (1 Thes. 5:21). I have no doubt there is a God in heaven who hears and answers the prayer for wisdom, grace, and deliverance from the evil one.

CHAPTER SEVEN:

FINISHING WELL

It's been said that getting old isn't for sissies. The older I get the more I agree. Every new decade of life has its challenges. The lust of the eyes, the lust of the flesh, and the pride of life are very real issues regardless of age. Temptations do not leave just because I have my 60th or 70th or 80th birthday. If anything, the tempter has a few new tricks to pull out of his bag. Sometimes, the things of earth that at one time were strangely dim begin to renew their luster. No, I don't think there is any age when you can take off your armor, lay down your weapons, and quit fighting the good fight of faith.

My favorite warning came from a good friend and mentor named Holman Johnson. All who knew him called him Uncle Johnnie. He founded a great camp in northern Michigan called Camp Barakel. At a Men's Retreat in the fall of 1996, Johnnie had just led us in singing a great old hymn of the faith. At that time he was in his eighties. He went to sit down and I proceeded to the pulpit. Just before taking his seat he said he wanted to say something to the men. He then made this statement "few old men finish well" and sat down. I was speechless. In what seemed like an eternity God paraded through my mind a multitude of saints who didn't finish well. I know of pastors who could preach circles around me, who know more scriptures and had better theology but who finished horribly. I know of other men and women who served the Lord faithfully for years that later became castaways. The scriptures record some big hitters who, likewise, didn't finish well.

NOAH

Noah was a man of faith and a preacher of righteousness. His example of faith convinced his family to believe the promise that God was about to judge the entire earth. They labored tirelessly on the ark for over 100 years because they believed it was their one and only way to escape God's wrath. The flood came and all mankind was destroyed except Noah and his family. The rainbow appears, the covenant is given, and an offering is made. Yet the last scriptural record of this seasoned veteran saint is that he got drunk, got naked, and cursed his son. He didn't finish well.

MOSES

Moses was a man who truly knew God. His journey of faith began as an infant rescued out of the Nile and raised in the palace of Pharaoh. He spent years tending sheep in the desert until the day he encountered God in the burning bush. He returned to Egypt a man of destiny. His role in God's wondrous redemption of Israel from Egypt would forever leave a mark on him. He led them through the Red Sea but he wouldn't lead them into the promise land. He had struck the rock the second time and forfeited the privilege of leading Israel to their homeland. The last words of Moses in the Pentateuch were, "And Moses was an hundred and twenty years old when he died; his eye was not dim, nor his natural force abated" (Deut 24:7). When he sought God's glory for himself and in his pride struck the rock, he was unable to finish well.

SAMSON

Samson is my favorite Old Testament Bible character. I think he typifies most American Christians. We have been born with a silver spoon in our mouth, spiritually speaking. Like Samson, we have had more than our fair share of opportunities to know and follow God.

Samson was one of only two perpetual Nazirites from his mother's womb. The other one was John the Baptist, of whom Jesus said, there was never a greater prophet born of woman, (Matt 11:11). It is my personal opinion, that if Samson would have walked with God, his accomplishments may well have made all the ministries of other Old Testament saints stand in the shadows.

Within his twenty year ministry, only two of his prayers are recorded. The first he prayed just after he had slain a thousand Philistines with the jawbone of a donkey. He was very thirsty, and called on the Lord and said, "Thou hast given this great deliverance into the hand of thy servant; and now shall I die for thirst, and fall into the hand of the uncircumcised? But God split an hollow place that was in the jaw, and there came water out of it, and when he had drunk, his spirit came again, and he revived" (Jud. 15:18-19).

His final prayer came at the end of a very sad life. A small lad led him into the pagan temple of the Philistines. There he was, a slave to the very people he was suppose to have conquered. He asked the boy if he could just feel the great pillars upon which the temple stood. "And Samson called unto the Lord, and said, O Lord, remember me, I pray thee, and strengthen me, I pray thee, only this once, O God, that I may be at once avenged of the Philistines for my two eyes. And Samson took hold of the two middle pillars upon which the house stood, and on which it was borne up, of the one with his right hand and of the other with the left. And Samson said; Let me die with the Philistines. And he bowed himself with all his might; and the house fell upon the lords, and upon all the people who were in it. So the dead whom he slew at his death were more than they whom he slew in his life" (Jud. 16:28-30). The man, whom God intended for great things, bore little evidence of prayer. He lived a shameful life with many regrets and died suicidal. He didn't finish well.

SOLOMON

Solomon was a man who knew God. The first half of his life bears evidence of a rich and intimate relationship with God. He unselfishly asked God for a wise and understanding heart that he might know how to lead his people. He diligently gave oversight to the building of the temple. He penned Holy Scriptures, preached powerful sermons, and prayed powerful prayers. His humble prayer at the dedication of the temple reveals much of his reverence for the only true God. He repeatedly instructed the people if they drifted away from God, they should humble themselves and pray. God gave divine confirmation of his prayer by sending fire from heaven and consuming the burnt offering. The glory of the Lord then filled the house and even the priests had to step back to a safe distance.

Prayer is our spiritual thermometer. Prayerlessness is usually one of the first steps a man takes in backsliding. Solomon's second half is quite another story. "For it came to pass, when Solomon was old, that his wives turned away his heart after other gods: and his heart was not perfect with the Lord his God, as was the heart of David his father. For Solomon went after Ashtoreth, the goddess of the Sidonians, and after Milcom, the abomination of the Ammonites. And Solomon did evil in the sight of the Lord, and went not fully after the Lord, as did David his father. Then did Solomon build a high place for Chemosh, the abomination of Moab, in the hill that is before Jerusalem, and for Molech, the abomination of the children of Ammon. And likewise did he for all his foreign wives, who burned incense and sacrificed unto their gods. And the Lord was angry with Solomon, because his heart was turned from the Lord God of Israel, who had appeared unto him twice" (1 Ki. 11:4-9).

The book of Ecclesiastes is filled with the pessimistic words of a cynical old man, who with many regrets has drifted far away from God. Solomon looked at his life and summed it up in his introduction. "The words of the Preacher, the son of David, king in Jerusalem. Vanity of vanities, saith the Preacher, vanity of vanities; all is vanity" (Eccl. 1:1-2). He no longer let God run his heart, but he let his heart run his life. Everything his heart desired he tried. His prayer life declined and his sins increased. You may ask how you know his prayer life declined, because humble people pray, and proud people do not. Proud people, if rich, are vulnerable to trusting in their riches. God had given Solomon wisdom, power and great wealth. Only great and deep communion with God in prayer could have salvaged him from the caliber of temptation he experienced. Oh how dangerous it is to live off yesterdays grace. He didn't finish well.

YOU CAN FINISH WELL!

JOB

"There was a man in the land of Uz, whose name was Job; and that man was perfect and upright, and one that feared God, and shunned evil" (Job 1:1). He was a man that prayed for his family continually. He went through horrible suffering when the devil assaulted his life. His ten children were all killed in one day, and his wealth was taken away by thieves. Yet, he said, 'The Lord giveth and the Lord taketh away, blessed be the name of the Lord.' His body was afflicted with a satanic outbreak of boils from head to foot. His wife caved in under the strain, and said, 'Even God can't help you now, curse God and take your own life.' Job's theology, however, remained strong, 'do we receive only good at the hand of the Lord and not adversity?' Three friends turn into miserable comforters and tormented him with false reasoning. God questions him at his lowest point and he responds humbly and repents in dust and ashes. God knows Job is a man of prayer so he instructs the three friends to go and have Job pray for them. Job prays and God blesses his latter end more than his beginning. He finished very well.

DANIEL

The book of Daniel is usually considered a book of prophecy. But Daniel is also a book of prayer. When

Nebuchadnezzar threatened to destroy all his counselors unless they told him the dream as well as its interpretation, Daniel knew to pray. He gathered his three companions together and they asked God for mercy. He not only revealed the dream and its meaning, he laid out the divine history of future kingdoms. God did all this in response to their prayer. Daniel consistently prayed three times a day. He followed the instructions of Solomon, who said, if Israel was ever in captivity, face Jerusalem and ask God to return the captives. Daniel knew a law had been made forbidding prayer to anyone but the king, but this was a time when he had to serve God rather than man. He was put in the lions den and God delivered him. At the end of his life he is again found praying, fasting, and confessing his sins as well as the sins of his fathers. The angel Gabriel appeared to him and had him write down words concerning the end of time. He didn't understand, but God said, it was ok and told him to shut the book and go his way. "But go thou thy way till the end be; for thou shalt rest, and stand in thy reward at the end of the days" (Dan. 12:13). He finished very well.

THE APOSTLE PAUL

The apostle Paul was a man of prayer. "For God is my witness, whom I serve with my spirit in the gospel of his Son that without ceasing I make mention of you always in my prayers" (Rom 1:9). Paul encouraged the churches to pray without ceasing, (1 Thes. 5:17). "Be anxious for nothing; but in everything by prayer and supplications with thanksgiving, let your request be made known unto God" (Phil. 4:6). To the churches of Ephesus he writes; "Praying always with all prayer and supplication in the Spirit, and watching thereunto with all perseverance and supplication for all saints" (Eph 6:18).

At the end of his life he is in prison for the gospels sake. He writes his last words to Timothy. "I charge thee therefore before God, and the Lord Jesus Christ, who shall judge the living and the dead at his appearing and his kingdom; Preach the word; be diligent in season and out of season; reprove, rebuke, exhort with all longsuffering and doctrine. For the time will come when they will not endure sound doctrine; but after their own lust shall heap to themselves teachers, having itching ears; And they shall turn away their ears from the truth, and shall be turned unto fables. But watch thou in all things, endure afflictions, do the work of an evangelist, make full proof of thy ministry. For I am now ready to be offered, and the time of my departure is at hand. I have fought a good fight, I HAVE FINISHED MY COURSE, I HAVE KEPT THE FAITH" (2 Tim. 4:1-7). I believe there is no better way to be ready to depart than to be prayed up. Paul had prayed his way through the slug fest of faith and could say, "I have finished my course, I've kept the faith."

"I have been young, and now am old; yet have I not seen the righteous forsaken, nor his seed begging bread" (Psa. 37:25). Oh Lord, our concern is not that you would forsake us in our old age, but that we in our old age might forsake thee. "...for he hath said, I will never leave thee, nor forsake thee" (Heb 13:5). May we finish well like the apostle Paul and not like Demas who left Paul having loved this present world, (2 Tim 4:10).

Closing thought: Only God knows what lies ahead in any of our lives, but regardless of what it may be, I believe the greatest contribution we can make to finishing well, in spite of our age, is to learn to pray. Oh God, may we learn to watch and pray at least an hour a day.

Manufactured By: RR Donnelley
                     Momence, IL USA
                     July , 2010

CPSIA information can be obtained at www.ICGtesting.com
Printed in the USA
BVOW05s1300131014

370534BV00002B/3/P